BIBLICAL MEDITATION & DEVOTIONAL

4 FEBRUARY

28 DAYS OF GOD'S ABIDING PRESENCE

BY CALLUM COKER

THE FREEDOM MESSAGE: PROVERBS LARGE

PRINT EDITION

THE PURPOSE OF LIFE

Introduction

The Bible is God's manual for life and love. A ROAD MAP CENTRED ON LOVE. The more we meditate on the promises of God's goodness the more our worldview is shaped by the God that heals and redeems rather than the false god's that bring your attention away from the healer and redeemer of our souls. This devotional is Christian based – God centred and God infused with truth in its corners, its centre and its titles. There are Bible verses, applications to the verse and prayers that bring a wholeness to meditating on God's word in this devotional.

I hope you enjoy this devotional as it was intended to help connect you to Jesus so you can be a light in your families, communities and nation.

February 1st

Day 1

Psalm 23:1

"The Lord is my Shepherd, I shall not want."

Insight: This iconic verse of scripture is well known throughout the world not only in Christian communities, it is often quoted in battlefields and in funerals, it implies that we as Christians take on the likeness of sheep In need of direction, that God in fact provides and leads his sheep, this verse is easily memorized but not often meditated on but it could be meditated on for centuries and truly not capture the depths of it's theological sharpness and grace, it's words are timeless. It's in the Bible for a reason; it heals the soul and leads you to Jesus and that is worth mediating on. Meditation is something we all do but meditating on Jesus brings lasting fruit both now and in eternity. We were designed with the Kingdom in mind.

Application: Throughout my day am I being self-willed or am I being led by the shepherd and trusting Jesus? Am I trusting in me, myself and I or am I being trusting like a sheep of the one who leads you into green lush pastures.

Prayer: Lord, help me to not lean on my own strength but let you guide me into your perfect will. Help me to be the vessel of hope that you want me to be and not worried with my eyes on the storms in front of me but the shepherd who guides me into the fullness of life. You are my Lord and healer. I trust you. Thank you for your unending goodness.

February 2nd

Day 2

Philippians 4:13.

"I can do all things through Christ who gives me strength."

Insight: Doing life in your own strength is the most normal way of living for the person devoted to life in the flesh and away from God's Holy Spirit. The Holy Spirit is our anchor in times of storm and gloom and Christ came to present a path of hope that gives us strength for the daily activities of our life

Application: When you have a tough or menial task that you do during your day will you ask for the Lord's strength to overcome the challenge or will your lean on your own strength.

Prayer: Dear Jesus, give me your strength not my own way, my own will and my own thoughts about what I need or do, I'm here for you, for your purposes for your glory. Grant me this day so that

I may be sculpted by your grace and used for your purposes in Jesus name Amen.

February 3rd

Day 3

Isaiah 40:31

"But those who hope in the Lord will renew their strength. They will soar on wings like eagles; they will run and not grow weary, they will walk and not be faint".

Insight: We can hope in all kinds of things some rooted in Biblical truth some are not even close to that reality. Christ came and conquered sin and death so that we could be whole and not be fragmented beings but deeply connected to his source of life. Eagles have a way of seeing above the storms he desires for us to be like eagles and sore. That is a mighty promise, eagles are graceful, and they have a way of commanding their space with authority and flair this is a direct picture of what is available for us in Christ.

Application: When you feel like there is no hope for the future quickly thank God that his resources are limitless and his love is unending, picture Jesus on the cross in your mind then see yourself placing your rogue thoughts that are not acquainted with his love and mercy placed on his shoulders then practice the art of righteous belief that you are the 'righteousness of God in Christ Jesus.'

Prayer: Dear Jesus, thankyou that I belong to you, thank you that I am a son washed in your precious blood, and I can walk in a new way held by Your love. Today is a new day and I choose you above all else to walk with me through the vicissitudes of this life.

February 4th

Day 4

Proverbs 27:19

"Just as water mirrors your face, so your face mirrors your heart."

Insight: It has been said that your eyes are the windows of your soul but your face is actually a mirror of your heart, this poignant piece of scripture is for our benefit and from the perspective of love. It is taken from Eugene Peterson's The Message translation. If you take care of your heart feed it the right nutrients of grace and wisdom this is going to result in a positive outlook on your facial demeanours. This is a net positive for anyone who wants to look great and cancel their Botox appointment, beauty in the Kingdom is always first inward before it shines on the outside. Beauty by the worlds standards are outside and very rarely do the examine the inner life. For us as Christians we sync into God's rhythm, calendar, timetable and way of thinking before we are conditioned by the world around us where as the world are always looking to the outside God is after the heart and the heart is the true source of life.

Application: When you prepare for your day take a moment to check your heart and build layers of hope there, picture Jesus smiling back at you as you take this step into his care rather than relying on the care that this world has to offer apart from him. Then get on with your day.

Prayer: Dear Jesus, thankyou that you have given me your word to be a world changer to reshape the world around me with your goodness anchoring my movements. Thankyou that I am loved by you even when I least expect it, thankyou for second, third and fourth chances. Thankyou that you are mighty in battle and a refuge for all those who are needing your care. Thankyou Jesus, Amen.

February 5th

Day 5

Ephesians 6:12-13

"For our struggle is not against flesh and blood, but against the rulers, against the authorities, against the powers of this dark world and against the spiritual forces of evil in the heavenly realms. Therefore put on the full armour of God, so that when the day of evil comes, you may be able to stand your ground, and after you have done everything, to stand."

Insight: The natural realm is often the senses that we are trained to use and operate out of, sight, touch, hearing but God has given us spiritual sight, spiritual hearing and he wants us to be connected as humans that have an affinity to the spiritual realm that is rooted and established in

Biblical truth. Thinking like heaven means taking the time to meditate on the thoughts of heaven and a great way to do that is by practicing the art of thankfulness and then pulling down the strongholds that would rob you of a full life in Christ. Standing against the devil and his schemes means standing in your authority as cleansed and being authoritative against the Kingdom of darkness due to Jesus defeat of sin and death on the cross. The armour of God is what is used to propel our offensive strategies and give us padding so we can attack darkness without fear, as a former cricket player we wore padding so that we could attack bowling at high speed without fear of getting hurt as we were protected and we are to be protected as Christians by the shalom and presence of God in this world that needs his light and truth.

Application: Picture the armour of God syncing into you and the river of forgiveness flowing through you and step into the plans and purposes of God with boldness. When you feel a hint of fear or dread picture the sword of God's truth swatting that away and then rest in the Bible verse 'The Lord is my shepherd' for comfort.

Prayer: Thankyou Jesus that you are with me, that you care and you are for me even when I'm not for myself, thank you that you gave me the weapons of God that encompass your word and Holy Spirit to defeat the schemes and strategies of the evil one. Thank you that I am alive, blessed, forgiven, made whole and a valued warrior for your Kingdom. Thankyou Jesus. You're awesome, Amen.

February 6th

Day 6

Psalm 42:1

"As the deer pants for streams of water, so my soul pants for you, my God."

Insight: We are supple creatures and God wants us flexible to his will, like the deer sips water for nourishment and strength. God has given us a timeless asset in his word to strengthen us in his presence so that we can counter the obstacles that life throws at us with care and joy. Appetites are a God given gift and they can be deployed for good or evil. Saul had an appetite for God that was set on the Jewish law but once he encountered God and became Paul his appetite was fulfilled in God's presence via the gateway of grace. Building an appetite like the dear for the streams of living water of God's word will provide strength for you throughout the day and in every endeavour you pursue.

Application: Take a moment to read your Bible, read until you feel your heart resting on a verse and then stay there for a moment and meditate on the promise allowing the word to sync into your heart and mind. Now you can run your race like the deer freely and with a spring in your step.

Prayer: God, thank you that you have given me a timeless jewel that I can ponder on in your word, I'm better for spending time in your word and can meditate on your goodness day and night. I'm getting better each day with your grace because of what Jesus did for me on the cross.

FEBRUARY 7TH

DAY 7

Isaiah 41:10

"So do not fear, for I am with you; do not be dismayed, for I am your God. I will strengthen you and help you; I will uphold you with my righteous right hand."

Insight: Fear is something we all have to contend with it is part of the human condition. What is fearful for one person is sometimes thrilling and worthy of adventure for another. Having a fear of dangerous situations is a good thing as a bad situational environment can cause significant damage but God in this verse is calling his people to relational trust and with that trust ensures a breaking down of irrational fear. Christ wants to raise up saints not push down sinners and by taking the time to know you are in Christ you begin to see the world as it was meant to be, a battleground where you are victorious.

Application: Picture your worst fear in your mind then ask Jesus to come in and take over the scene watch as he fills you with faith to confront the impossible with his grace and love.

Prayer: Christ you are sure and steadfast, a very present help in times of trouble and I need you to show up. I call forth every obstacle that is hindering me from your calling over my life to broken and removed as I trust you. I know that I am loved and that you are truly good. Thankyou Jesus, amen.

FEBRUARY 8TH
DAY 8

Hebrews 11:1

"Now faith is confidence in what we hope for and assurance about what we do not see."

Insight: Faith is undoubtedly a core pillar of the Christian faith, that is why it is called the Christian faith. Another word for faith is belief and believing in religion won't save you but being in relationship with God will give you the power and abiding presence to overcome any and every obstacle, we need to realise and be grounded in that truth as we pray, attend church. Ask the Holy Spirit to help you throughout your day as we are building blocks of faith that will help and bring us forth into the fullness of life that Christ purchased for us on the Cross.

Application: Spend a moment to picture yourself as confident with Jesus alongside you as you step out into your day, picture yourself communicating certainly and with people who want to hear what you have to say, picture yourself a saint who has overcome shame, guilt and condemnation by God's grace.

Prayer: Father I thank you that today I am with you, that you sent your son to die for me on the cross that I could live whole and free with no qualms about who I am or what I'm supposed to be, you lead and I follow, that's the order, you are a God of breakthrough, blessing and more than enough. I trust you fully. Thank you that I walk in faith as a child of the Most High God. I Bless you in Jesus name, amen.

FEBRUARY 9TH
DAY 9

Ephesians 1:18

"I pray that the eyes of your heart may be enlightened in order that you may know the hope to which he has called you, the riches of his glorious inheritance in his holy people."

Insight: Some people struggle with their eyesight that's why they get glasses so they can see better, more clearly. Christ has given us spiritual sight that operate like glasses so they can see clearly. The spiritual realm is alive and well and some people can see into it and others are blinded because they haven't been to see the eye specialist yet, in this case getting spiritual sight is not something that you can conjure up in your own strength or purchase at your local supermarket. Spiritual sight is found in connection with God. The imagination is a wonderful weapon of God's armoury for his saints and many people refuse to develop their imagination with righteous intent. Guarding your imagination with the pillars of scripture and prayer will ensure the pictures that you form in your imagination are Holy, blessed and bring structure to your day and lives.

Application: Picture yourself in your dream home, dream relationship, a church that is flourishing, a job that is fulfilling and friends that understand and care for you then bring Jesus into the centre of your situation and let him tidy up your life piece by piece so the gap between what is and what will be is redeemed so that Christ is given permission to work on your behalf and with you to see your dreams and his dreams come together.

Prayer: Thankyou Jesus that you are a redemptive God that the worst of our today's become like putty in your hand that you mould to shape a masterpiece, no matter how bad things get we can still come to you and you accept us as we are and reshape us into the vessel that you intended for us to be.

FEBRUARY 10TH
DAY 10

Proverbs 10:28

"The prospect of the righteous is joy, but the hopes of the wicked come to nothing."

Insight: The world promises that sex, drugs, alcohol and fame will bring joy and success but nothing could be further from the truth. The true source of Joy is from God, believing in God, believing in what he says and doing what he says. The Holy Spirit, God's word and connection to Christian community is a great way to understand the ways and life rhythms of joy that can be discovered in your everyday life. If you are walking contrary to God's ways there is no hope that your plans will succeed because Christ has been absent from your thinking and methodology. This verse is clear that if you want a brighter future get close to God and believe what he says and joy will be the byproduct of your heart commitment and relationship to him.

Application: Write down 10 things that the world promises will bring fulfilment then write out 10 truths from God's word that counter those false statements so you can counter the enemies lies with the beauty and wisdom of God's truth.

Prayer: Thankyou God that you gave us Jesus as the true source of joy. Jesus is the redemption of our lives and King of our hearts. Thank you that you came down from heaven so that we could know you fully and be able to experience joy not as a doctrine that is replaceable with religious dogma but true lasting joy.

FEBRUARY 11TH

DAY 11

Psalm 121:7-8

**"The Lord will keep you from all harm
— he will watch over your life;
the Lord will watch over your coming
and going both now and forevermore."**

Insight: One of God's qualities is he is a protector, he shields, he guides, he gives us the keys that we need to survive and thrive with his help. Christ is the lifter of our heads and healer of our souls. It is crucial to note that not all of life is going to go our way but when we surrender to him we are beginning to live on the right track. Once God blesses, you are blessed and there is nothing Satan can do to rob you when you are cocooned in Christ's presence, he may try to make you feel inferior but you belong to Almighty God. When you step out into new territories or adventures - God is with you, he shepherds, and he gives you the strength to fulfil the calling that he has uniquely designed for you.

Application: Imagine your greatest enemies all coming at you, then picture Jesus brought into the centre of the situation, watch him remove these enemies one by one and then let him hold you and shield you from attack as you lean into his strength.

Prayer: Thankyou Jesus that the life of faith is one that I don't have to battle or strive to obtain on my own to obtain your blessings. You are a God of overflow and abundance. You are a protector and have given me the heart of your kid to blaze new trails and leap over walls that would stop or hinder me from outworking your magnificent calling in my life. Today is a new day and I choose you to live in and through me. Thanks Jesus, Amen.

FEBRUARY 12TH
DAY 12

Matthew 11:28

"Come to me, all you who are weary and burdened, and I will give you rest."

Insight: This verse is one of my favourite and one of the first verses that I ever memorized, why I connected with this verse so easily was because of how relatable it was to the truth that was in my heart that life creates burdens that require us to either keep piling up burdens or releasing them into God's care. I choose the path of applying forgiveness and releasing them into God's care. Jesus wants us to live a life that is not separate from him in any way so in every way we can give him thanks and trust him to produce the fruits of the Holy Spirit in our life where there has been dullness, pain and drudgery. This verse is the words of Jesus himself and presents a way to deal with your burdens, releasing them to Jesus.

Application: Imagine all of the things that are weighing you down and make you feel like you aren't achieving your best results. Then place those burdens on the cross so you can walk in freedom.

Prayer: Dear Jesus thanks for second, third and fourth chances, thankyou that I can hear from you clearly and you can take my burdens and place them before you where I know you love and seek to restore me to the fullest version of myself. Thank you that you paid the price for my freedom and that walking with you is the best life possible, keep me focused on you and your ways so I can bring honour to your name, In Jesus name I pray, Amen.

FEBRUARY 13TH
DAY 13

Isaiah 42:6

**"I, the LORD, have called you in righteousness;
I will take hold of your hand."**

Insight: We have a consistent scattering of choices available to us as humans, all competing objectives of what is actually important. Jesus takes our hand, this is an offer of friendship but also trust, he wants us to be friends with him but also to trust in his goodness. Jesus forgiveness is permanent but he has also called us to come out of sinful habits and to walk in a brand new clean way that is centred on hope and sanctification, to live correctly you need to know God's word and you need to welcome the Holy Spirit to be a permanent resident in your life and welcome his hope and tuition to repaint and decorate your life as he sees fit. This process isn't always an easy one as old habits can conflict with this new nature. Jesus best for us is righteous living not lawlessness that is held back by the flesh. Satan wants you stuck in cycles of torment that are connected to the flesh, Jesus desires the opposite one of freedom and eternal impact that rests in his goodness. This devotional is a great step in realigning the mind with God's promises so you can be a positive impact to the world around you.

Application: I desire you Lord to be my friend and to walk in righteousness as I know my positional righteousness is secured thanks to your son who bled and died on the cross so that I can be free. I trust you, I choose you, help me to walk in my identity as a son and chosen. Thankyou Jesus for your consistent love, Amen.

FEBRUARY 14ᵀᴴ
DAY 14

Romans 5:5

"And hope does not put us to shame, because God's love has been poured out into our hearts through the Holy Spirit, who has been given to us."

Insight: A flow on effect of hope is influence. False hope is not healthy and it comes at a cost to your time and effectiveness but authentic hope is grounded in God's goodness and never ending love. The Bible says 'hope deferred makes the heart sick but a longing fulfilled is a tree of life.' Shame is ultimately rooted in bad behaviour and condemnation this is juxtaposed to the grace that is poured out when connected to the Holy Spirit. When a jug is poured, it is not a few droplets - there is an abundance of water and God wants you to know that he is the provider of more than enough. This verse is a call to intimacy with God first then action not action absent of God's presence. God desires that we build with him.

Application: Picture the worst thing that you have done and then hand it over to Jesus, watch him throw it on top of the cross and walk away free, that is the beautiful exchange of sin to righteousness when you receive Christ.

Prayer: Thankyou Lord that you are a God of blessing, you exchange our weaknesses for your strength and you let us soar above the here and now with your wisdom that brings cutting edge ideas into reality. I ask you, release new insights to me for my day so I can be a blessing to those around me, thanks Jesus, Amen.

FEBRUARY 15ᵀᴴ
DAY 15

Psalm 119:114

**"You are my refuge and my shield;
I have put my hope in your word."**

Insight: So many people trust in all kinds of things, their favourite sports team, a political party or politician or a friend to bring them a sense of security, trust and hope in anything but God is the only path to authentic security is only found in God. The Psalmist knew that life threw a myriad of distractions that could take away his hope. He spent time in God's word because he knew that through Christ he had clear direction and a way forward that would make sense to his Spirit that was being trained into the art of life producing light and direction from heaven's internal GPS. David knew the Holy Spirit before the Holy Spirit was poured out in the Book of Acts because God's word is timeless. In the movie 300 the Spartans are being attacked by a barrage of arrows on the battlefield, they put up their shields to defend themselves from the arrows that are being flung at them from a distance and at incredible speed. They are defended and safe, they are ready to fight again. This is what the anchor of God's word and presence offer, a safe space from enemy attacks. This verse is one that is powerful and should be one that is mulled over and memorized for victory in daily life.

Application: Imagine you are in a fortress where nobody can get to you and you have God's word, then recite this one verse then in the corner of this fortress is a sword and a shield you are then sent out into the scene in 300 where you are part of the Spartan army ready to battle the Persian army that are corrupt and evil. You have righteousness, a sword of truth and victory before you in everyday life. As a Christian you are now a warrior in this current day for God's kingdom and God's glory.

Prayer: Today is a new day and I bless you Lord, every day you are good and I choose to make you my refuge and trust in your goodness, give me the courage to be like the Spartans that fought the

Persian army bravely in 300 for their community, way of life and freedom. Lord I pray that I can fight the good fight with a humble spirit, joy and life giving hope. Thankyou for all that you are, thankyou for your love that never falters, you are truly good and truly care about me, I give you praise and I delight in your presence, thanks Jesus, amen.

FEBRUARY 16TH
DAY 16

Psalm 130:5

**"I wait for the Lord, my whole being waits,
and in his word I put my hope."**

Insight: Patience is a virtue of the Holy Spirit that we often overlook within the context of the fruits of the Spirit, Joy, kindness, love they tend to get quite a lot of attention but patience is crucial because God is a builder and building takes time. So Patience is something that is worthy of note. God is with us, he gives us time and then he expects us to redeem it with him building the life that he desires so we can leave a legacy that points people to Jesus. Our time on this planet is limited and God wants to be known to us and be King of our lives. Hope is what gives you the fuel to step out and do new things, faith gives you the certainty that God is involved and you can have a clear mind. Forrest Gump waited at the bus stop with a joyful expectation of good that he would see his beloved Jenny, while he was waiting he was telling stories of his life recounting the good and the lessons learned. Like Forrest while we are waiting for God's deliverance in our lives and his dreams fulfilled we need to be mediating on the good that God has done in our lives and be ready for his love to wash over us and give us a fresh perspective that rises above our circumstances and releases the sounds and sights of Heaven.

Application: Watch the scene on YouTube of Forrest Gump telling stories of his life at the bus stop, imagine you are there and that Jesus is sitting right next to you, then begin recounting the good that God has done and continues to do and then ask Jesus where were you when these events happened and let him reshape the scene and reshape your future with Christ immersed in your life in the past, present and future.

Prayer: Father in the name of Jesus I thankyou that today I can learn patience, I can practice the joy of your presence and live from your amazing grace, I bless you because you are good. I thankyou that all of life is founded in you and I can live life to the very full because of who you are. Every day you are good, everyday I can look to you and trust in your hope for my salvation for my freedom for my deliverance because of what you accomplished on the cross for me, help me to be like Forrest Gump, tender hearted and responsive to the opportunities that are in front of me while looking to your love as I wait for your blessings to be manifest in my life. Thankyou Jesus it is in your mighty name I pray, Amen.

FEBRUARY 17TH
DAY 17

1 Peter 5:6–7
"Humble yourselves, therefore, under the mighty hand of God so that at the proper time He may exalt you, casting all your anxieties on Him, because He cares for you."

Insight: Humbling doesn't mean timidity or quietness it is boldness in God's promises, David was humble when he faced Goliath, he knew that God's word was being challenged and the people of God were being troubled by this giant who was claiming to take the Israelites off the turf that belonged to them. Goliath was defeated because David was humble enough to know his God. Humbling is dependence on God and trust in his word and ways and often the flesh and former habits that contradict God's truth will compete with this new pattern of living but God has a way of dealing to the rubbish in our lives and securing an unquestionable victory. God is good that is rock solid truth. Living in his truth will result in blessing that is also truth. Truth sets the saints free not error and error bombards our mind consistently in this world.

Application: In what ways have you been trained to think differently than the Biblical standard that God presents in his word. Write down beliefs that compete with God's truth then bring the truth into the light through God's word. Allow his truth to set you free today.

Prayer: Father I thankyou that you are a God of truth and that as we humble ourselves we can experience the favour of God on our lives. I am thankful that I get the gift of today to make changes to my life and be a world changer in my family, community and nation. Thankyou for your word that is a priceless jewel that redeems, sets free my patterns of disastrous thinking, then helps me to live in alignment with the will and purpose of heaven. In Jesus name I pray, amen.

FEBRUARY 18TH
DAY 18

Psalm 37:5

"Commit your way to the LORD; trust also in him; and he shall bring it to pass."

Insight: Planning is not a demon, it is a good thing to plan and prepare and rely on solid planning principles and routines. We plan to eat, we plan to work, we plan to achieve outcomes that are positive and leave a lasting impact. We plan to be new creations in Christ Jesus. This is good, very – very good but plans need to be supple and presented to God for his thoughts, his editing, his approval, by design God is good and we can trust that his adjustment in our lives are for our betterment and for his glory and this is very positive. Jesus is a God of order and cares, he wants to release into our care his blessings today. Sometimes our dreams do not line up with his dreams and that is why rejection isn't really rejection it is preparation for the next thing so we can develop and be better. There can be ad hoc results from not being prepared so we need to ensure that we live lives that are mouldable to his will and not determined to go against it when we have the wrong ideology or processes that God cannot bless.

Application: Write down three goals for today that you didn't think of before this meditation. Allow them to sync into your subconscious and believe you can achieve them with your will and conscious decision to move towards that righteous goal.

Prayer: Father. I thank you for the gift of free will and that I can choose to deploy that gift for your glory. Thankyou that you are a God who cares and is trustworthy and that I can walk in freedom. I have devoted myself to your love and am in right standing with you because of your son. Thankyou Jesus and I bless you for you are truly mighty and good. I thank you in Jesus name I pray, Amen.

FEBRUARY 19TH
DAY 19

Psalm 147:3

"He heals the broken in heart, and binds up their wounds."

Insight: Brokenness is part of the human condition but Jesus came to heal our brokenness so that we can live whole lives in his presence. Once a wound is healed the area is often stronger and such is the case with soul wounds once we heal up we are wiser and have more understanding. I have been through heartache but through it I have learned valuable lessons, the pain wasn't wasted and it has taught me to lean into the person of Jesus as my anchor for all that is life. Jesus is close to the broken hearted because we were designed to live passionate lives with our hearts connected to the work and calling that we chase after and live from. The great minds of artists have well developed hearts because it is from the heart that their gift is sustained and gives them the love that they need to carry on doing the work that they do and the line between play, work and adventure is often blurred in this beautiful mystery held in the soul. Guarding your heart with God's presence and healing your heart with God's presence is the way forward. God will never tire of us coming to him and leaning on his grace, mercy and wisdom. He's a loving Father and healer, it is just what he does.

Application: Picture you are on a seesaw, on one side of the seesaw is your worst experience that you can remember and on the other side of the seesaw is you steering at this funky pile of rubbish, then all of a sudden Jesus enters the scene and he takes the rubbish and throws it on the cross and begins to play with you on the seesaw, you can now play with Jesus, talk to him about your experiences and live connected to his wisdom in a brand new way that allows your worst moment to be a school for others and now a testimony of God's overcoming and sustaining power.

Prayer: Thankyou Jesus that you heal the broken-hearted, that you are a God of imagination and colour and you have released timeless treasure through your word, thankyou for a new day a brighter day and your healing presence that covers and sustains. Thank you for your love. You are truly good and there is nothing you cannot do to release your goodness and joy in my life. Thanks Jesus, amen.

FEBRUARY 20TH

DAY 20

Matthew 6:31–34

"So do not worry, saying, 'What shall we eat?' or 'What shall we drink?' or "What shall we wear?' For the pagans run after all these things, and your heavenly Father knows that you need them. But seek first His kingdom and His righteousness, and all these things will be given to you as well. Therefore do not worry about tomorrow, for tomorrow will worry about itself. Each day has enough trouble of its own."

Insight: This is a collection of a few verses for our daily meditation for February but I feel it is necessary and we will examine them together. Worry is a time waster, and a joy breaker and Jesus wants us to defeat worry with the truth that God provides and worry can now be fully absent in the life of the believer and saint, thanks to Jesus and the abiding presence of the Holy Spirit that heals, restores, delivers and sets us free for all eternity. People who do not know Christ chase after sex, salary and status, fame and the allure of the flesh but the true treasure is living from God's voice and trusting him to provide, to shelter, to love and cherish you. He will but it is a paradigm shift that needs to be monitored by his word, Christian community and the beauty of a praising lifestyle drenched in prayer. Seeking first the Kingdom means that we are to live from a heaven to earth paradigm not a paradigm from earth to heaven. In other words, Christ lives in us and through the Holy Spirit and Jesus positional status as being seated at the right hand of the Father, a victorious King, so we have insights into living from heavens throne that can only be released by people who live in connection with the King of Kings. Jesus wants us first to co-create with him from Heaven's blueprints.

Application: List a few of the things that you worry about and then place them before Jesus and watch these things as they transfer into juicy fruit that Jesus now chomps on before you and becomes the fruit of the Spirit, teaching us patience, joy and kindness so we can impact the world around us with grace.

Prayer: Thankyou Jesus that you don't leave us as orphans but that you equip us to live victorious lives in the communities that we live in and bring the truths of your word into focus so we can be shining lights in the world. Thankyou for who you are and what you have called me into. I can trust you and your promises and know that you are good even when life doesn't make sense. Teach me about your kingdom and how not to worry by setting my gaze on the heavenly realm. I pray all of this in the mighty name of Jesus, amen.

FEBRUARY 21ST

DAY 21

Psalm 36:7

**"How priceless is your unfailing love, O God!
People take refuge in the shadow of your wings."**

Insight: Jesus love never fails, that is as true as it gets when it comes to Christian doctrine. The word priceless here contains the thought that his love cannot be purchased, there is no dollar value that can capture the beauty of God's word to us. We are Christians because we put Christ first. Christ is the anchor for our lives not the side hobby that the religious cling too in order to be part of a club when it was relational closeness and fellowship that God designed us for. Wealth is a blessing but riches is not, wealth is generational, riches are collected and spent on fleshly pursuits.

The phrase 'shadow of your wings' implies that we are seeing from a heavenly perspective above the here and now as we make Jesus our hearts trust and then we can release the sounds, sights and wisdom of heaven over our communities. Jesus wants us to soar like eagles, will you let him shield you as you soar?

Application: Imagine you're flying above your city on a gigantic eagle seeing life as God sees it, then you see Jesus on another eagle right next to you, let his thoughts for the city you are in permeate your mind and jot down any spontaneous thoughts you have to heal the community that you are apart of with Christ's wisdom and grace.

Prayer: Father, I thank you that you are a healer, that you are wisdom personified and your love knows no bounds. You are truly King and Lord. Thankyou that you remove demonic strongholds placed in my path and that you pave the way for a brighter future, there is nothing in my past that you cannot atone for and redeem and nothing in my future that is beyond your ability to build with me as your co-creator on this planet. Let me build with you, let me love like you and let me know your love in a brand-new blessed dimension.

Thank you for your mercy and grace, in Jesus name I pray, amen.

FEBRUARY 22ND

DAY 22

Proverbs 3:5–6
Trust in the LORD with all your heart, and do not lean on your own understanding. In all your ways acknowledge Him, and He will make straight your paths.

Insight: This is an iconic verse in scripture and is one that I definitely recommend is memorized so that it is safely stored in your heart. Jesus doesn't just want bits and pieces of your heart, the Sunday praise rhythm or the chat after church you have with your pals, he wants your dreams, your desires, your waking moments and the moments that hurt, he wants to strengthen you in his presence so that you can be effective in the world that is consistently competing with the words of God and the truth of scripture for your affection and seeks to rob you of the hope that you are called too.

Application: Write down three areas where your life is not fully trusting of God, then write down three verses and prayers that release trust to God who is sovereign, who you can trust in these areas and realise your potential.

Prayer: Thankyou God that I can know you and be known by you, thank you for your blessings and even the tough moments that I don't understand so that I can learn and trust you.

FEBRUARY 23RD

DAY 23

Isaiah 42:8
**"I am the LORD; that is my name!
I will not yield my glory to another
or my praise to idols."**

Insight: The word 'Lord' implies ownership, think of landlord, they own the property but you get to enjoy using the property for your living purposes as a person who rents. This is symbolic of the type of relationship that we get to delight in with Jesus. He is the owner of our life yet we still get to love it and express our talents, hobbies and gifts in the everyday life. Idols are often subtle because they start off with a suggestion from the satanic realm that is sneaky and it is diametrically opposed to the wisdom and truth of scripture. Yielding implies choice, that there are forces pushing you in a direction that is not conducive to the Holy Spirit of God and this is something that we need to be aware of as Christians that we have a triune enemy of the world system, the flesh and the devil and we counter the temptations of the flesh with the word and spirit of God and believing the truths of God's word that belong to us as sons and daughters of the living God.

Application: Jesus wants to remove idols that compete with our life. Ask the Lord to reveal to you idols in your life and seek to destroy those idols once and for all by removing them from your life and replacing them with the biblical habit of sound thinking and praise to Jesus.

Prayer: Thankyou Jesus that you are a kind and loving saviour but you are also jealous and desire for us to be fully committed to you. You are not only good you are great and there is nothing to disastrous that you cannot consume with your love and truth. Teach me to do your will and live in accordance with your love. In Jesus name I pray, amen.

FEBRUARY 24TH

DAY 24

Psalm 34:1

**"I will extol the LORD at all times;
his praise will always be on my lips."**

Insight: The art of thankfulness needs to be a consistent theme in the life of the believing Christian. Thankfulness draws our hearts and minds to God and then God releases his love and thoughts into our minds as a testimony of his goodness, he comforts us in our pain but what thankfulness does its work it fills our hearts with God and begins to remove the shackles of shame and guilt that stifle, crush and imprison grace filled vessels of hope that he desires for us to be and become.

Application: Listen to a praise song on Spotify, listen to it again and again and let the lyrics of adoration to God centre your thoughts so you can be filled with his praises.

Prayer: God thankyou that you are alive that you know me, that you care for my every need and that you are with me through the storms and good times in life, I can understand you and walk into the best life possible as I cooperate with your word and tutelage. I'm redeemed and can walk in the lifestyle of a saint for your purposes, I pray for all those who are hurting right now that they will know this God of comfort like I do and that Christ's name will be glorified always and for all time in my life.

FEBRUARY 25TH

DAY 25

Psalm 35:28

"My tongue will proclaim your righteousness, your praises all day long."

Insight: Words matter, how we deliver words matter, it was by God's word that the earth was formed and the heavens. Christ had a way of delivering his healings and miracles by words. Words create marriages, words tear down marriages, words create, words bless and words curse. If you have a problem of leaning towards the negative the psalmist has your cure in this verse: PRAISE! This singular weapon against the problem of wrong thinking develops fresh pathways in your brain that changes your thinking to believe in God's word and his promises over your circumstances. We need to confront circumstances but from a posture of victory and grace not brokenness and defeat. The Psalmist praises all day long so this is a rhythm of his life, thanking God and allowing his joy to be manifest in his life for God's glory and Kingdom advancement. The more we are aware of God's presence the more that we can shift the atmosphere around us from unbelief into God belief that removes mountains and establishes Christ's Kingdom. A glory Kingdom of hope and influence.

Application: Write down 10 things that you would like to see breakthrough in your life in the next 10 years and then begin claiming the righteousness of God in your life so that you can step into all that God has for you in the next season of your life. Keep a notepad close by for any fresh thoughts and impressions that the Holy Spirit releases to you as gems of insight that can help you achieve these goals.

Prayer: Father I thankyou that you are King, that you are Lord of the universe that you have laws that are fully realised in the person of Jesus and I can fully know him in this life so that I can live in freedom and grace as a byproduct of your goodness. Thankyou Jesus for your love that secures my hope in a strong foundation and that is the person of Jesus Christ who made a clear way for me to be in right relationship with the Father, thankyou for your Holy Spirit and I pray for your peace to be evident in my life in a fresh way so I can increase in discernment and wisdom.

FEBRUARY 26TH

DAY 26

John 16:33
"In the world you will have tribulation. But take heart; I have overcome the world."

Insight: Not everything is going to go your way, that is a fact of life. There are challenges, we have a very real enemy in Satan who 'roams around like a roaring lion seeking whom he may devour.' God wants to give us the keys to life eternal and to remove the pain of our yesterday with the hope of a brighter tomorrow. That's who God is, he is a redeemer and giver of hope and life. We don't have to live in fear as Christians we can choose to live in the presence of God. The world competes with God's word all the time. The world says you need to be a Billionaire to be successful, Christ says you need to give from what you have. The world says that fornication is the normal and fun. Christ says I've called you to a life of purity and covenant that is meaningful and builds a holistic connection that encompasses Body, Soul and Spirit. The world says that marriage is now redefined to mean any gender and not between male and female. God says I've made both male and female for a purpose and I don't make mistakes, you're valuable and you have a purpose that only you can fulfil. The world says that if you don't fit into our culture you are an outcast. Christ says, you are a champion and a warrior for what is true and right, noble and Holy and you will be comforted by my presence and know my love in a deeper way.

Application: Pick up a newspaper write down 10 lies that are presented by journalists that contradict God's word then google bible verses on the topic and write down the corresponding truth to counter the lies of ideology that shame and condemn people. Then thank Jesus that you have the gift of discernment and God's presence to decipher what is truth and what is error.

Prayer: Thankyou Jesus that you are my refuge, that I can come to you in my brokenness and realise your love for me in new ways everyday. Thankyou for your love that conquers all and that you have defeated all enemies of authentic love on the cross. Thankyou that you paid the price on the cross for my sin so that I could live in freedom.

FEBRUARY 27ᵀᴴ

DAY 27

Philippians 4:6–7
Do not be anxious about anything, but in every situation, by prayer and petition, with thanksgiving, present your requests to God. And the peace of God, which transcends all understanding, will guard your hearts and your minds in Christ Jesus.

Insight: Anxiety is the antithesis of trust and trust is the natural state of believing In Christ and the outworking of tangible faith that heals. When a mother bird is sheltering a bird in a storm, the little bird doesn't bother about the storm it is cocooned in the presence of her mother bird and the baby bird knows that it is safe under the shelter of her mother, we are meant to live in this realm of safety and trust under the shelter of Jesus

Christ. Jesus is alive, he has strategies for our welfare and his ways are good. These are truths that are designed to be etched into your heart not robbed from us in cruel ways through fowl thinking. Within this verse are keys to be living in a brand-new realm of breakthrough and that is praise and prayer. Praise and prayer defeat the enemies of worry and living that counter the truth of God's word. God didn't come to earth to make living obscure and a maze that you couldn't find out, he declared that he is 'the way, the truth and the life.' The outworking of praise and petition to the throne room of God is peace which is the manifest presence of God realised in your life.

Application: Write down 10 things that you are worried about in your life. Then spend 10 minutes in praise thanking God for victory over these fears and worries and petition God for his blessing and victory over these areas of concern. Then spend a few minutes tuning to your heart and welcoming the peace of God that is promised in this verse for the saints of God.

Prayer: Father in the name of Jesus I thankyou that I can live in your peace that it is not some obscure and aloof concept but a felt reality that I can live in and from all the day s of my life, thankyou that you are truly good and that you do what you say and that I can and will trust you with my life. Thankyou for your blessings that chase me down and I bless you in the mighty name of Jesus, amen.

FEBRUARY 28TH

DAY 28

1st CORINTHIANS 13:13
"And now these three remain: faith, hope and love. But the greatest of these is love."

Insight: Faith, hope and love are core pillars of the Christian worldview. Faith in Christ, hope for a better tomorrow and the love of God expressed to you, through you to change the world around you in alignment with God's plans and promises. Faith without love brings brokenness and hope without love brings no outworking of the hope that you so desire and long for. Blessing is connected to these three qualities and living in the blessing of God's unending goodness require love, faith and hope all working together in your life. The anomaly of faith, hope and love is that faith, hope and love are not separate from one another. They interlap and are woven together to create an integrated wholeness. This creates unstoppable momentum in a life and is what provides a hope for the future that is blessed so that you can work and live in a way that is meaningful and releases Kingdom impact. Faith, hope and Love are qualities that need to be cultivated through praise, worship, biblical meditation and self-forgiveness. We all mess up but God doesn't and he took our blunders and placed them on the cross for our victory and to establish a continuous supply of victories in our lives.

Application: Write down 3 things that you have faith will come to pass that line up with goals that are in your heart and within the guidelines of biblical desire. Write down 3-character qualities that you want to develop over the next 5 years and then imagine yourself achieving these dreams as hope realised and love expressed in your life.

Prayer: Thank you Jesus that you died on the cross for my freedom, that I can live in connection to you that you are a healer, deliverer, life giver and you catch my worries and turn them into beautiful testimonies that radiate your joy and deliverance, thankyou that blessings chase me down because I am connected to you and blessing is what you do, it's who you are, a life affirmer, truth co-ordinator and Kingdom builder. I pray for all those who do not know you that they may come into connection with your love and experience your goodness in their life. It's in Jesus name I pray this prayer, amen.

FIN

ABOUT THE AUTHOR

Callum Coker is a Christian who is passionate about pursuing the Holy Spirit, connecting people to Jesus in the context that they live in and seeing this planet become the 'Heaven on Earth' reality that is available for individuals, communities and nations. This project is one in a series of books that will explore the curiosity he has for creativity and imagination whilst holding close the pillars of sound Theology and artistic expression through his work. Callum likes sports, reading and playing guitar. When he's not doing these recreational pursuits, he likes to spend time with friends, family and work on his next project, whatever that may be.

www.ingramcontent.com/pod-product-compliance
Lightning Source LLC
LaVergne TN
LVHW051428080426
835508LV00022B/3297